JOHNNY WINTER PLAYS THE BLUES

BY TOBY WINE

Recording Credits:
Johnny Winter, Lead Guitar
Paul Nelson, Rhythm Guitar
Dave Rubin, Bass

Cover photo by Mark Weis

Cherry Lane Music Company
Educational Director/Project Supervisor: Susan Poliniak
Director of Publications: Mark Phillips
Publications Coordinator: Rebecca Skidmore

ISBN 978-1-60378-149-7

Visit our website at www.cherrylaneprint.com

CONTENTS

About this Book 3

About the Author 3

Acknowledgments 3

Introduction 3

A Select Johnny Winter Discography 4

Blues Essentials 5

The Licks 11

   Tonic Licks 11

   IV–I Licks 17

   Turnaround Licks 22

   Codas 28

   12-Bar Solos 31

Slide Licks in Alternate Tunings 36

   Open G Tuning 37

   Open D Tuning 42

   "Open F♯" Tuning 45

ABOUT THIS BOOK

Johnny Winter Plays the Blues explores the art of blues soloing by examining the work of this unquestioned master of the style. Whether you are a beginner or a seasoned blues musician, you will reap the benefits of Johnny's expertise, accumulated during a lifetime of devotion to this vital art form. Chapter by chapter, we'll break down the 12-bar blues form and learn vocabulary, technique, and harmonic approaches that will take your playing to new levels of depth and authenticity.

ABOUT THE AUTHOR

Toby Wine is a native New Yorker and a freelance guitarist, composer, arranger, and educator. He is a graduate of the Manhattan School of Music, where he studied composition with Manny Albam and Edward Green. Toby has performed with Philip Harper (of the Harper Brothers and Art Blakey's Jazz Messengers), Bob Mover, Ari Ambrose, Michael and Carolyn Leonhart (of Steely Dan), Peter Hartmann, Ian Hendrickson Smith, Melee, Saycon (currently starring in *Fela!* on Broadway), Tobias Gebb, and the Harlem-based rock band Kojomodibo Sun, among others. His arrangements and compositions can be heard on recordings by Tobias Gebb and Unit Seven (*Free at Last*, currently in the jazz top 10 nationwide), Phillip Harper (*Soulful Sin, The Thirteenth Moon*, Muse Records), Ari Ambrose (*Early Song*, Steeplechase), and Ian Hendrickson Smith (*Up in Smoke*, Sharp Nine). Toby leads his own trio and septet, does studio sessions, and works as a sideman with a variety of tri-state area bandleaders. He spent four years as the music librarian for the Carnegie Hall Jazz band, and is currently an instructor at the Church Street School for Music and Art in Tribeca. He is the author of numerous Cherry Lane publications, including *1001 Blues Licks, The Art of Texas Blues, 150 Cool Jazz Licks in Tab, Steely Dan: Legendary Licks*, and *Dave Matthews Band Under the Microscope*.

ACKNOWLEDGMENTS

Many thanks are due to Cherry Lane's head honcho, John Stix, and to my friend and editor, Susan Poliniak, for her insight, guidance, and absurdly patient good nature. Additional thanks to the extended Cherry Lane family for all that they do so well. Thanks as well to my parents, Rosemary and Jerry, and to Christina (C-Ups), Bibi, Bob, Jack, Noah, Enid, Mover, Humph (R.I.P.), fellow author Karl Kaminski, and all of the great teachers I've ever had.

INTRODUCTION

Johnny Winter is revered by guitarists and blues aficionados the world over for his virtuoso playing and unmatched knowledge of the style and its history. The Texas-born Winter began his musical career on clarinet and ukulele, but quickly switched to the guitar and became a local teenage sensation. His earliest influences were the great players of the Chicago scene, and he paradoxically grew more enamored of the many legendary Texas bluesmen only after he'd moved away. However, he recalls that he "listened to everything" and studied the work of Muddy Waters, T-Bone Walker, Lightnin' Hopkins, Elmore James, Robert Johnson, and others diligently. With his brother Edgar on keyboards, he recorded his first tracks at the age of 15 and continued to cut his teeth playing club gigs and doing session work in Texas and neighboring Louisiana. His 1969 major label debut for Columbia Records, *Johnny Winter*, showcased the fascinating style he dubbed "progressive blues" and ran the gamut from acoustic slide work to incendiary electric soloing while also featuring his soulful and charismatic vocals. By the time he'd released his second album and appeared at the Woodstock music festival, Winter was a certified star whose music always kept one eye on the future and the other focused squarely on the rich blues traditions of the past. In the years that followed, he continued to release critically acclaimed albums that mixed select covers of blues classics with original material that fused rock and blues styles seamlessly. His 1976 release *Captured Live!* featured a now-legendary performance of Bob Dylan's "Highway 61 Revisited," and in 1977 he lived his dream as he produced and collaborated with his idol, Muddy Waters, on the Grammy-winning *Hard Again*, the first of a series of records documenting their partnership. As the decades have passed, Winter has turned increasingly to traditional blues. He is passionate about his stewardship of this vital American art form and continues to spread the message of the blues with every note that he plays.

A SELECT JOHNNY WINTER DISCOGRAPHY

Johnny Winter (Columbia, 1969)

Second Winter (Columbia, 1969)

Johnny Winter And (Sony, 1970)

Live Johnny Winter And (Columbia, 1971)

Austin Texas (a.k.a. *The Progressive Blues Experiment*) (United Artists, 1972)

Still Alive and Well (Columbia, 1973)

Saints and Sinners (Columbia, 1974)

John Dawson Winter III (Blue Sky, 1974)

Captured Live! (Blue Sky, 1976)

Nothin' But the Blues (Blue Sky, 1977)

White Hot and Blue (Tristar, 1978)

Raisin' Cain (Acadia, 1980)

Guitar Slinger (Alligator, 1984)

Serious Business (Alligator, 1985)

Third Degree (Alligator, 1986)

The Winter of '88 (MCA, 1988)

Let Me In (Virgin, 1991)

Hey, Where's Your Brother? (Point Blank, 1992)

Live in Houston, Busted in Austin (Magnum, 1994)

Live in NYC '97 (Point Blank, 1998)

Back in Beaumont (Magnum, 2000)

I'm a Bluesman (Virgin, 2004)

Johnny B. Goode (Carlton, 2005)

Raised on Blues (Blues Boulevard, 2008)

Live at the 2009 New Orleans Jazz and Heritage Festival (MunckMix, 2009)

Blues Essentials

While it's beyond the scope of this book to teach you *everything* you need to know about playing blues guitar, this chapter may help by detailing some of the techniques and materials essential to the style. Some or all of this information may already be comfortably under your fingers, in which case you may proceed to the next chapter or refresh yourself as you see fit. If you're new to the style or see anything with which you're unfamiliar, take some time to get a firm grasp on the material that follows. You won't get far without it.

Scales

While there are a tremendous variety of scales and modes available to the soloist in nearly every harmonic situation, there are a handful that are employed so frequently in the blues style that their importance cannot be disputed. First and foremost is the minor pentatonic scale, shown below in the key of G.

G Minor Pentatonic Scale

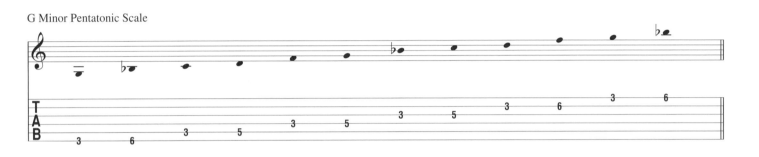

If you've been playing the guitar for more than a few days, it's likely that you're familiar with this scale; it's often the first thing a player learns and it's used extensively in rock, blues, jazz, and country styles. This is a *moveable* scale form, meaning that there are no open strings involved and it can be moved around the neck to fit whatever key you're playing in. If you need an A minor pentatonic scale, simply shift everything so you begin the scale with your index finger on the 5th fret rather than on the 3rd fret. Notice that I've included the high B♭ in the diagram above, going past the root (G). This note occurs on the low E string so there's no reason not to add it in on the high E string as well. Often, the minor pentatonic scale is supplemented by the addition of the ♭5th in both octaves, as shown below. This new scale is often referred to as the *blues scale.*

G Blues Scale

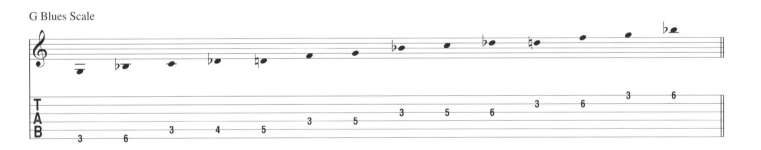

It's vital when playing scales such as these that you stay in position unless there's a reason to move. For instance, you should play all 3rd-fret notes above with your index finger, and all 4th-, 5th-, and 6th-fret notes with your middle, ring, and pinky fingers, respectively. Admittedly, many rock and blues guitarists avoid using the pinky and instead stretch with their ring fingers to get to higher notes such as those on the 6th fret in the above example. However, pinky strength and independence should be developed as much as possible—it's on your hand, so why not use it? In any event, many players who stretch with their ring fingers often reach even further with the pinky to get to higher notes, so it's not as if they're ignoring this finger entirely.

The minor pentatonic and blues scales may already be familiar to you, but do you know how to play them starting on the A string? The diagrams below illustrate these scales in what may be a new fingering for you.

G Minor Pentatonic Scale with Root on A String

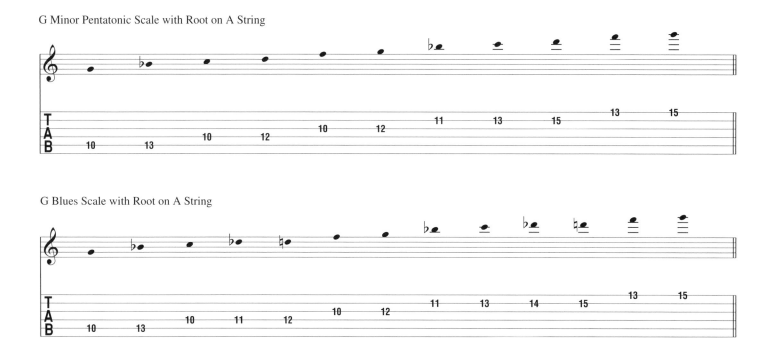

G Blues Scale with Root on A String

As you can see, these new fingerings greatly increase your range and ability to move horizontally across the neck rather than keeping you locked into the "blues box." At the very least, they can give you somewhere to go when you want to climb into higher registers during a solo. Note that in the scales above, you begin in 10th position (i.e., your index finger plays all 10th-fret notes), but you'll have to shift up to 11th position once you hit the B string.

Another essential scale in the blues is the major pentatonic. While the minor pentatonic scale includes the root, ♭3rd, perfect 4th, perfect 5th, and ♭7th degrees, the major pentatonic scale includes the root, major 2nd, major 3rd, perfect 5th, and major 6th. The diagrams below illustrate the G major pentatonic scale, beginning on both the low E and A strings.

G Major Pentatonic Scale

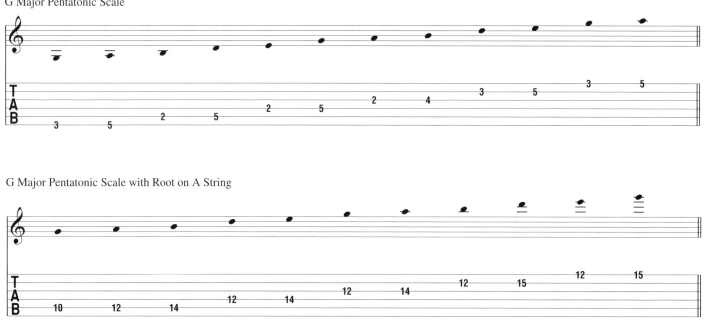

G Major Pentatonic Scale with Root on A String

The major pentatonic scale beginning on the low E string should start with the *middle* finger so that you are in 2nd position when playing in G. There are a few different ways to approach the A-string fingering, but many players find it easiest to start with the index finger and then slide over two frets to play the rest of the scale. In the example at the bottom of page 6, you would start with your index finger on the 10th fret of the A string and then shift over two frets to play all of the 12th-fret notes with your index finger, and the notes on the 14th and 15th frets with your ring and pinky fingers, respectively.

As you work your way through this book, you'll see that Johnny Winter constantly mixes notes from both minor and major pentatonic scales to create his licks. It's a practice as old as the music itself, and the dichotomy of minor and major together is at the heart of the style. Try different combinations of the two scales and come up with some licks of your own. It will take a bit of trial and error to discover which combinations sound the best to you and are most stylistically correct, but careful examination of Johnny's lines will reveal some of the most typical and authentic arrangements of these tones.

Before we move on, let's take a moment to discuss an experienced blues musician's approach to soloing with these scales. We'll stick to the key of G for now. The first four measures of a 12-bar G blues should be played over a G or G7 chord. During this time, you would play any combination of notes from the G minor pentatonic, blues, or major pentatonic scales. When the chord changes to C or C7 in measure 5, you may remain on the G minor pentatonic or G blues scale, or move up to notes from the C major pentatonic scale. The C minor pentatonic and C blues scales *should not be played here*, mainly because the E♭ present in each of these scales would be too jarring. With the return to the G chord in measures 7 and 8, you should use the same approach for this chord as earlier in the form. With the arrival of the D or D7 chord in measure 9, you may stay with the G minor pentatonic or G blues scale, or move up to a D major pentatonic scale. Follow this by moving down to C major pentatonic in the next measure or simply returning to the G minor pentatonic as you finish out the 12-bar form. Confused? Take a look at the chart below.

Measure	Chord*	Scale Choice
1–4	G	G minor pentatonic G blues G major pentatonic
5–6	C	C major pentatonic G minor pentatonic G blues
7–8	G	G minor pentatonic G blues G major pentatonic
9	D	D major pentatonic G minor pentatonic G blues
10	C	C major pentatonic G minor pentatonic G blues
11	G	G minor pentatonic G blues G major pentatonic
12	D	D major pentatonic G minor pentatonic G blues

*May be a triad, 7th chord, etc.

Shifting scales on the fly like this may take some getting used to, but it's an important skill for navigating the chord changes effectively. Yes, you could just wail away on the G blues scale the entire time, and many players opt to do this for the majority of their licks, but the finest practitioners of the style usually acknowledge the shifting harmonies beneath them in some way, even with simply a few choice notes here and there. For an easy introduction to this approach, stick with the G blues scale for the entire 12-bar form except in measure 9, with the move to the V chord (here, D). Shift to the D major pentatonic scale for this measure alone, and then return to the G blues scale for the rest of the chorus. This simple alteration will have a huge impact and will make for a much more interesting soloing style in the long run. After you've become more comfortable with these shifts and the new fingerings involved, you can ramp up the complexity even more with the addition of C major pentatonic notes in measures 5, 6, and 10. Johnny Winter employs all of these methods at one point or another in the licks in this book.

Shuffle and Straight Eighth Note Rhythms

The blues is played in just about every tempo and groove imaginable, be it old-school Delta blues, heavy rock, western swing, New Orleans second-line, funk, or what-have-you. The most important distinction to make regardless of the style is whether it is played with a straight eighth note feel or a "shuffle" feel. The former hardly needs explanation—each beat is divided exactly in half by eighth notes, and solo licks are played evenly as in many rock and funk grooves. The examples in the key of A in this book are all played in an even eighth note feel. The flipside of this is the shuffle or "swing" feel commonly used in traditional blues and jazz playing. In this feel, there is a constant undercurrent of eighth note triplets behind each quarter note beat that may be implied or explicitly stated by the bass, drums, and often the soloist. These triplets give each beat a sort of "loping" character that creates the shuffle feeling. It's not easy to describe a groove without hearing it, but essentially what is happening is that a group of two eighth notes are played as if they fell on the first and third part of an eighth note triplet. Take a look at the diagram below.

To help get the feeling down, try this useful exercise away from the guitar: Tap a steady stream of quarter notes with your foot at a moderate tempo. Next, tap a series of eighth note triplets on your knee so that there are three equal beats for every tap of your foot. Finally, omit the second tap of each three-note grouping per beat. Got it? That's pretty much how eighth notes should be played in a shuffle feel. Try playing this familiar blues riff, presented in each rhythmic style.

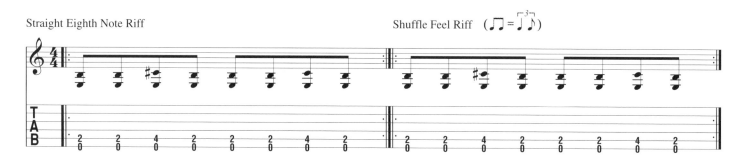

As with all things, it may take you a while to become comfortable with these two distinct grooves, but they should become easier to distinguish with time. Listen carefully to your favorite blues artists and take note of the feels they employ in various songs. The idea of triplet-based eighth notes is still only an approximation, and some players exaggerate or minimize their effect. Try to focus in on the way the bass and ride cymbal are used on recordings as well, as together they are the driving force behind any groove. With experience, you'll be able to hear and play this great music in any rhythmic style and at any tempo imaginable!

Bends

Blues guitarists bend strings to smear pitches and imitate the wail of the human voice. The bend is an essential technique, and one that should be familiar to you if you've been playing for a while. Nonetheless, let's take a moment to look at a few typical bending techniques you'll encounter in the pages to come. In the first example below, the B string is bent up a whole step from F to G to match the pitch played on the high E string above.

The bend should be performed with the ring finger, with either or both of the middle and index fingers lined up behind it on the B string to aid in the push towards the ceiling. This is what would be classified as a *pitch-matching bend*, and by playing the G on the high E string first, you give yourself a target pitch. Bending in tune is crucial, and missing your mark in terms of intonation can quickly brand you as an amateur.

Try the following pitch-matching bend on the G string, again with the ring finger pushing towards the ceiling. Use your middle finger to help exert some added force to the motion.

Those are by far the two bends most commonly encountered with the minor pentatonic scale, and in the entire blues style. Another oft-employed bend is the *pre-bend*, in which a string is pushed upwards to a specific pitch before being struck. This kind of bend is most commonly combined with a release back down, as in the example below.

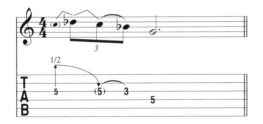

As you can see, the G string's 5th-fret C is pushed up a half step before the string is struck, and then the bend is released back down to its original position before you pull off to the B♭ at the 3rd fret. Pre-bends can be a little tricky, as you need to predict just how far to push the string without first hearing its pitch while bent. You'll likely find that each string—and, in fact, each guitar you play—requires varying degrees of force to pre-bend effectively and in tune.

Two other important types of bends are *oblique bends* and *unison bends*. In the former, two strings are struck simultaneously, and one string is bent while the other remains stationary. In the diagram below, the pinky is used to play the F at the B string's 6th fret, while the ring finger, assisted by the middle finger, bends the 5th-fret C up to D on the G string. The second time you perform the bend, release it back down and pull off to the B♭ while allowing the F to continue ringing above.

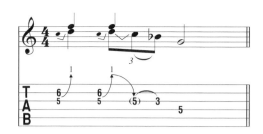

Finally, unison bends are similar to oblique bends in that one string moves while the other does not, but in this case, the lower note is bent to match the higher note exactly. In the example below, use your index finger for the high E-string notes and your ring finger (with middle-finger assistance) to push the B string up to match it. Unison bends will quickly reveal if your bends are in tune or not!

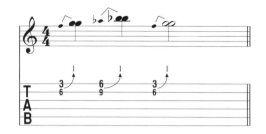

You'll have plenty of opportunities to explore these techniques in the licks to come. Johnny Winter uses them extensively in his playing, as do all of the major blues guitar stylists. Just don't overdo it—bends require a lot of finger strength and can leave you with sore hand muscles as your strength develops.

Philosophy

Let's take a moment to discuss a more philosophical approach to the blues and to the music in this book.

The blues is a genre of individualists and unique stylists, players who often lacked a formal education but found their own ways to innovate and leave their mark on the music. Study the living daylights out of Johnny Winter's playing, as it reflects the whole history of the blues through his own devotion and erudition. However, your ultimate goal should be the expression of yourself and not the mimicry of others, no matter how great they are. In the first days of recorded music, many players refused to have their work committed to wax, as they feared their ideas would be stolen by others—the greatest offense imaginable at the time. In the contemporary milieu, replete with iPods, instructional books, and college music programs, such a scenario seems quaint and antiquated. One need not be obsessively worried about such things, but the old-time attitude is still at least worthy of contemplation. We no longer exist in such a vacuum, but we still must assert our individuality lest we become pale imitators of past masters.

There are thousands of guitarists the world over who can spit out rapid-fire pentatonic licks for hours at a time, but the number of truly unique voices within the style is far, far fewer. By studying, for example, the work of Johnny Winter, you will gain a greater grasp of the techniques and vocabulary of the blues, and that is undeniably vital. This shared vocabulary—the product of decades of beautiful playing by your musical ancestors—will allow you to play with stylistic authenticity. One wouldn't think of writing a novel without first studying the English language and reading the work of the greatest practitioners of that art. The blues is no different. The novelist must have his or her own story to tell, and the same is true of the blues musician. You will ultimately want to tell *your* tale—not Johnny's, Stevie Ray Vaughan's, or Muddy Waters'.

Always remember that the blues began not as a forum for virtuoso guitar soloists, but for musical raconteurs who used the style to express their pain, love, triumphs, and failures. Look within yourself and unearth your own story. Then, share it with the world.

THE LICKS

All of the examples in this first part of the book (the second part being devoted to slide guitar licks, beginning on page 36) were recorded with Johnny tuning each of his strings down a whole step from standard tuning: D–G–C–F–A–D, low to high. Tune down accordingly if you'd like to play along with the recording.

TRACK 01

Standard tuning down one whole step, low to high: D–G–C–F–A–D.

TONIC LICKS

Let's examine a number of licks and phrases that fit over the tonic (I chord) and the first four measures of a typical blues.

All of the licks can be played in standard tuning as well, but the bends will be just a little harder to manage because of the higher string tension.

Let's start in the key of G. All of the licks in this key are to be played with a swing (shuffle) feel as described in the last chapter.

This first example is played primarily in 3rd position, meaning that all 3rd-fret notes are to be played with the index finger, all 4th-fret notes should be played with the middle finger, and so on. The A♭7 chords in the example should be viewed as *chromatic passing chords*: brief steps outside the key that make the accompaniment more interesting to play over but serve no real harmonic function. In other words, Johnny doesn't solo in A♭—the chords merely break up the rhythm guitar part so it's not just four straight measures of G7.

After the initial three-note pickup, the G string is bent up a whole step at the 5th fret, raising the pitch from C to match the D that follows on the B string's 3rd fret. Use your ring finger, assisted by the middle finger lined up on the same string behind it, to execute this and all other bends in the lick. The triplet phrase in measure 2 begins in the same way; try barring the B and high E strings with your index finger at the 3rd fret to play the notes that follow the bend. The second bend in the measure is a pre-bend, meaning that the G string must be pushed up a whole step *before you strike it*, and then released back down to C on beat 4. Measure 3 incorporates the major 3rd, B, and ends with a quick shift down to the A string's 2nd fret. The final two notes in the lick require you to slide up the B string to the 8th fret with your pinky, matching the Gs on the high E string's 3rd fret. Add a little vibrato by rapidly bending the B string up and down a short distance; go too wide and the effect will be more comical than expressive.

TRACK 02

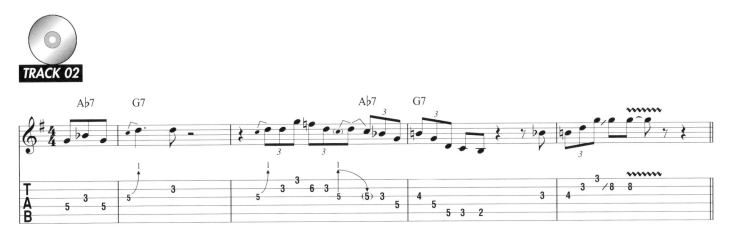

This next phrase uses triplets and repetition to great effect. Begin in 3rd position, hammer-on from the 3rd to the 5th fret on the B string, and then follow the 3rd-fret high E-string G with a slide into the B string's 8th-fret G. This kind of "pitch-matching" occurs frequently in blues and rock guitar styles, and takes advantage of the interesting timbral differences between strings. You may be playing a G in each instance, but the different thicknesses of the B and high E strings afford each of the notes a slightly altered texture that's appealing and highly idiomatic. The end of the phrase sends you up the neck to 13th position, with the ring finger taking all Ds on the B string. The D♭s in the final beat provide a nice descent towards the C that would inevitably follow in the next measure.

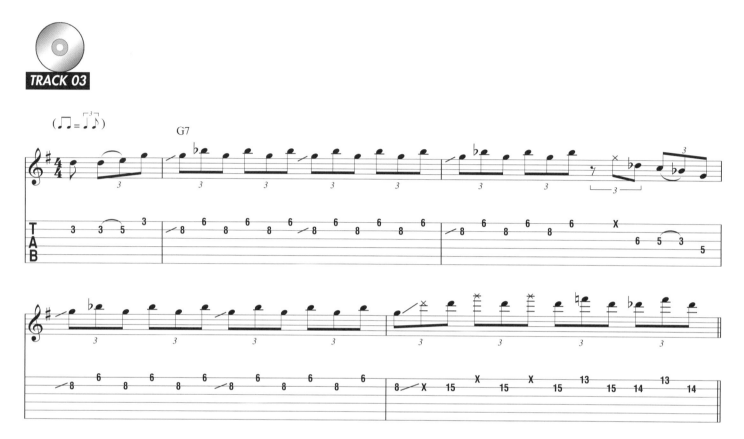

When Johnny plays, it's with an awareness of the whole history of the blues, and this encyclopedic knowledge informs his every phrase and solo. The lick below draws upon classic ideas of repetition and riffing in the traditional sense—punchy rhythmic ideas that are singable and accessible, gaining momentum with each new iteration. Play it strictly in 3rd position until the final measure, where you'll slide up the G string to the 7th fret with your ring finger, taking the Fs on the B string above with your middle finger. The double stops in the earlier measures should be played with your index and ring fingers barring the G and B strings at the 3rd and 5th frets, respectively.

The next lick closely mirrors the previous phrase but adds a few subtle variations. The initial bend pushes C up a half step to D♭ (the ♭5th) rather than D as in the first example. A pickup is added, and the open D string is struck briefly in the 1st measure. More importantly, Winter demonstrates that returning to strong thematic material can bring a sense of unity and cohesion to your playing. If you have a good idea, don't just play it once and forget it—bring it back and see what kinds of variations you can spin on it. Less is indeed often more!

TRACK 05

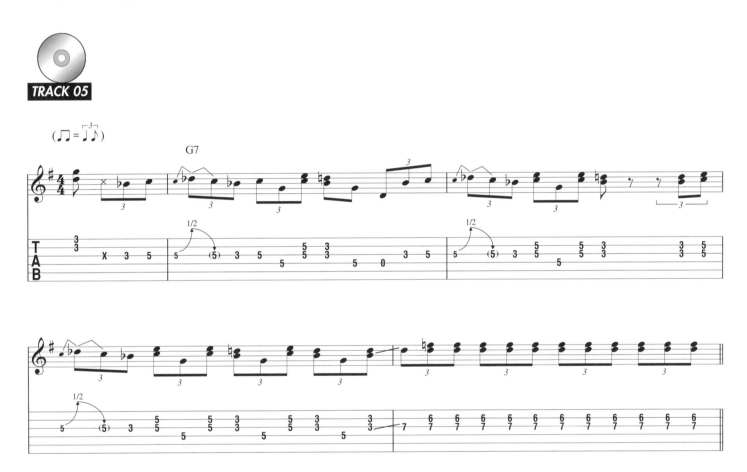

This next example is constructed primarily with three-note chords played on the G, B, and high E strings. It is essential that you learn these and the many other shapes and inversions possible on the upper strings if you want to play the blues effectively. A "top-down" view of chords, rather than one that looks up from the root, can enable a more melodic approach, so take note of the lead tones in your chords, as well as in the roots. After the opening single-note triplet, Johnny slides into repeated G7 chords that omit the root and put the 3rd, B, in the lead. In measure 2, he slides the shape over a fret—an old-school move that can be interpreted in a few different ways. If the bass stays on the tonic (G), the end result is essentially a G diminished chord (the A♯ is the minor 3rd, the C♯ is the ♭5th, and the E is the major 6th/diminished 7th). If the bass moves down with the chord above, it's simply a passing chromatic chord (G♭7). And, if the bass moves to the IV (C), the resulting chord becomes C7♭9 (C♯ becomes the ♭9th, E the major 3rd, and A♯ the ♭7th in relation to C). This drop down a half step is nearly always followed by a return to the opening chord, as in measure 3. The lick ends with a combination of two- and three-note chords in the upper register, which are played over a chromatically ascending sequence (G♯–A–A♯–B) that leads to the IV chord (C).

TRACK 06

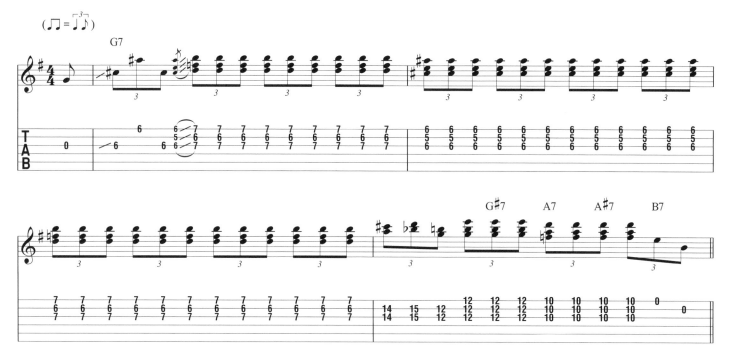

Here's a slick little bending lick that repeatedly pushes C up a whole step to D on the high E string. This bend should be performed with the ring finger (use the middle and even the index finger to assist). Rhythmic variety adds interest to the phrase and, in measure 3, the bend is released gradually downwards a half step at a time, first to D♭ and then to its original, unbent position at C. You may want to play both the D and D♭ before attempting the phrase to help ensure pitch accuracy. Nothing says "amateur hour" quicker than a handful of out-of-tune bends!

TRACK 07

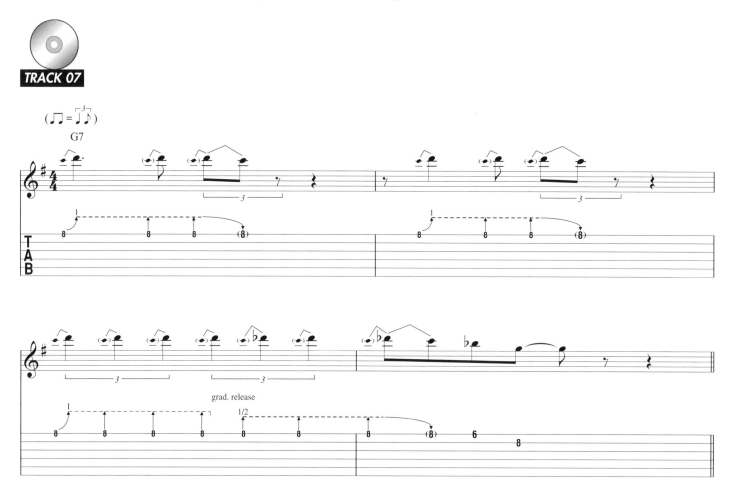

The next two licks are in the key of A and are played with a straight eighths feel—not swung. The first is to be played strictly in 5th position, although you will likely want to use your ring finger for both the 7th-fret G-string and 8th-fret B-string bends. These are by far the most commonly bent notes in the pentatonic and blues scales! The lick contains a number of pull-offs and the use of the ♭5th (E♭) in the final measure as well.

TRACK 08

The lick below has more than a few points of interest: repeated whole step bends-and-releases on the high E string (use that ring finger again!), the use of both the major and minor 3rd (C and C♯ over an A chord), and a half step shift upwards in the final two beats of the phrase. One can look at the latter as either a little bit of chromatic "outside" playing, or as the introduction of altered extensions to the A chord (D♯ is the ♯11th, A♯ is the ♭9th). Either way, these tones create an edgy sonority that must be resolved in the measure that follows. Stay in 8th position until you encounter these final five notes, and then use your ring finger to slide down the G string into 6th position to close out the lick.

TRACK 09

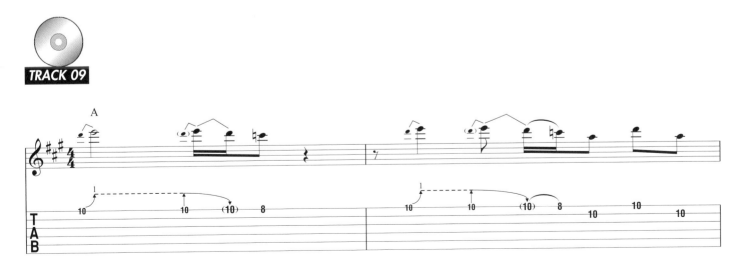

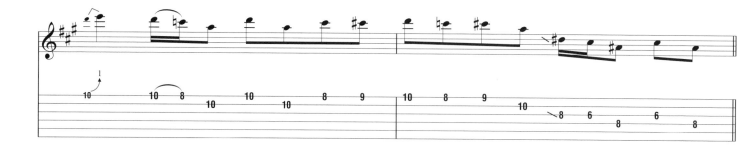

The final lick in this chapter is in the key of E and has a 12/8 time signature, meaning that each measure has 12 beats, with an eighth note (rather than a quarter note) lasting one beat. It's a common time signature for slow blues, and should actually be felt as if it were in 4 with a triplet on each beat—in other words, you don't need to tap your foot 12 times per bar! One of the beautiful things about this phrase is the way it combines soloing with its own accompaniment, alternating smoothly between high-register licks and low-register riffing. Begin with your ring finger on the B string's 3rd fret and perform the G-string bend that follows with your middle finger. After striking the open high E string, drop down and play the familiar riff pattern on the low E and A strings. In the final measure, use your middle finger to slide up the B string to the 8th fret and stay in this position as you close out the lick.

Any blues guitarist worth his salt should be able to sit down and play the style unaccompanied. Try using this straightforward example as a jumping-off point for some solo explorations of your own. Keep it simple, keep it rhythmic, and have fun!

TRACK 10

IV–I LICKS

In this chapter, we'll take a look at a handful of licks that can be used over the central four bars of the blues (measures 5–8) and the IV–I chord progression encountered therein. However, you should by all means explore the many ways in which all of the material covered in this book can be reinterpreted and employed in a variety of settings, including various places in the blues form, differing harmonic backdrops (chord sequences), and other styles entirely. One can and should develop a highly individualistic playing style by pulling from a wide swath of influences, as Johnny Winter and all the other blues greats have, creating a unique amalgamation of their predecessors and filtering it through their own artistic sensibilities.

Let's return to the key of G and the C7–G7 progression played in the middle of the 12-bar blues chorus. This first lick begins in 6th position with a three-note pickup leading into an 8th-fret, ring-finger bend on the high E string. After releasing the bend and pulling off to the index finger, finish the first measure and then drop down to 3rd position, where you'll remain until the very end of the lick. Notice how Johnny employs the major 3rd of the C7 chord (E) in measure 2, and then uses both major and minor 3rds (B and Bb) over the G7 chord in measure 3. While it's very common to play the minor 3rd over the tonic, *this interval is generally avoided over the IV chord*. In other words, stay away from Eb over a C7 chord unless it's a quick passing tone.

The next lick features some cool over-the-barline phrasing courtesy of a repeated five-note phrase played in an eighth note triplet rhythm. Begin by sliding up the G string with your middle finger, putting you in 8th position. The first five-note grouping begins on beat 2 and crosses over the barline into measure 2 during the second of its four iterations. After Winter rights the rhythmic ship, he moves back to 3rd position and ends the phrase with a tasty resolution on the major 3rd (B over G7).

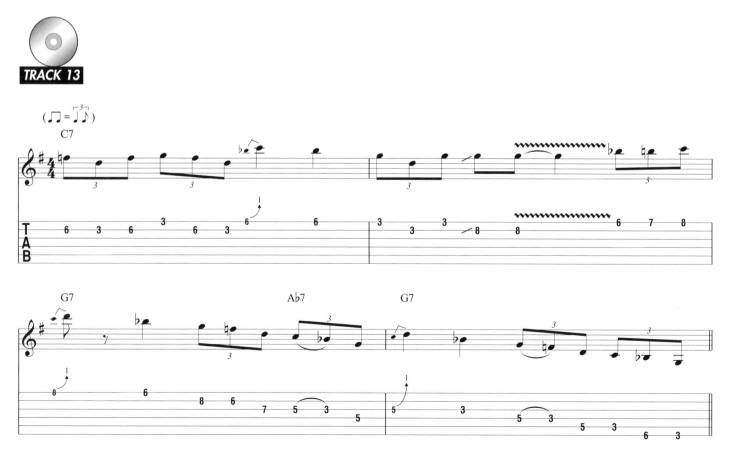

TRACK 13

The lick below begins in the 3rd-position, G pentatonic blues box and features a whole step, high E-string bend in the 1st measure. Some players use the pinky for this bend, but most would likely stretch a bit and use the stronger ring finger. It's this finger that should perform the B-string slide in measure 2 and the opening bend in measure 3 as well. On beat 4 of that measure, jump back down quickly to play the last three notes in 3rd position, and then finish out the excerpt with a ring-finger, G-string bend and a triplet descent down the G minor pentatonic scale.

This next excerpt is a pretty little phrase that features whole step bends from the major 2nd to the major 3rd interval on both C7 (D–E) and G7 (A–B) chords. The end result is a sense of sunny brightness that contrasts nicely with the more commonly heard minor 3rds and underlines the delicate balance between minor and major that is at the heart of authentic blues playing. The G-string slides in both the pickup and in measure 2 should be played with the middle finger, while all 10th-fret bends should be performed with the ring finger. Measure 3 includes a somewhat oddball chromatic climb from G to G# to A, while the final bar mixes notes from both the minor and major pentatonic scales (the major 3rd, B, and major 6th, E, in the latter case).

The lick below begins with a middle-finger slide up the G string into repeated double stops that combine the major 3rd (E) and 5th (G) of the C7 chord. In measure 2, drop down into 3rd position for a quick hammer-on/pull-off lick that uses the major 3rd and 6th (A) of the chord, and then slide up the B string with your ring finger to the 8th fret. The final measure begins with a grace note—a quick hammer-on from B♭ to B that is fast enough not to take any real measurable time—and then a return to 3rd position and another combination of minor and major pentatonic tones.

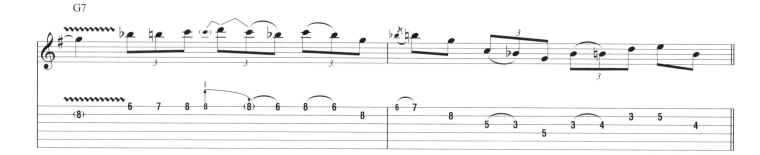

The final three examples in this chapter take us back to the key of A and a funky, straight eighth note feel. The IV–I progression is now D–A rather than C–G. You may notice that Johnny's three-note groupings throughout these licks are some combination of two 16th notes and an eighth note, rather than the eighth note triplets encountered in the G blues examples. It's a natural shift, as the triplet-based shuffle feel used in G naturally encourages triplet-based solo lines, while the straight feel in these examples practically discourages them.

Start this one in 8th position, performing the 10th-fret bends with the ring finger (again—it's by far the most common bending digit). Drop down into 5th position for the final beat of measure 2, and check out the way Winter once more combines major and minor pentatonic scales over the A chord. There are major and minor 3rds (C♯ and C, respectively), as well as the 9th (B) and the major 6th (F♯). The last tone could also be referred to as the 13th, as it's played in the upper octave. Remember, the 9th is equivalent to the 2nd, the 10th to the 4th, and the 13th to the 6th. We refer to these intervals with the higher numbers when they occur more than an octave above the chord root.

TRACK 16

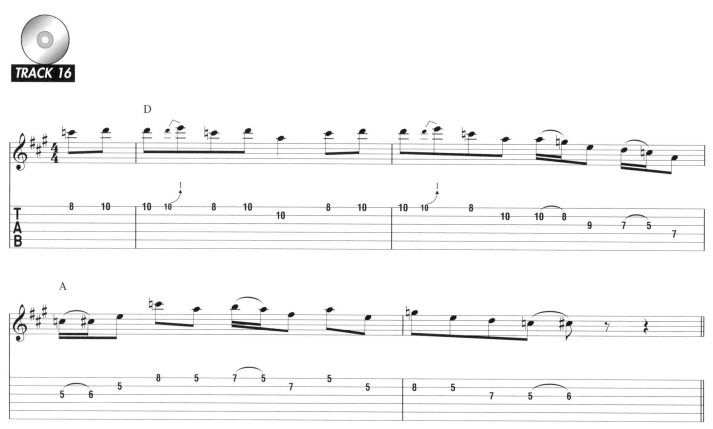

The next lick consolidates many of the ideas and techniques we've already observed into a nicely flowing, uninterrupted four-bar phrase. Once again, it's your choice whether to play all of the bends here with the ring finger or to enlist the pinky (on the 8th fret) as well, but don't leave 5th position at any time during the example. This is "box" playing at its best, making the most out of a confined space on the fretboard without cramming in 10,000 notes in the process. Rest assured that Johnny can and has done that kind of playing, but he also knows that there's no need to show off or prove himself. It's a good lesson for all of us to learn: Leave some gas in the tank and don't feel that you have to play everything you know every time you take a solo.

TRACK 17

The pickup for the final lick in this chapter begins with an octave jump up and across two strings from D (on the A string) to D (on the G string) and a whole step bend to match the E that follows. Slide up the B string with your ring finger in the 1st measure, and then use the same finger for the bend-and-release from A to B and back down again. Shift back to 5th position on the last beat of measure 2 and stay there for the remainder of the phrase. Once more, we get 16th and eighth note combination groupings and the use of upper extensions—the 9th (B) and 13th (F♯).

TRACK 18

TURNAROUND LICKS

In this section, we'll examine some of Johnny's choice licks and phrases played over what may be the most crucial part of the 12-bar blues form: the last four measures, or *turnaround*. Most commonly, this will mean V–IV–I–V with each chord lasting for one measure, although variations are common. There are a whole host of harmonic possibilities that may be either played explicitly or implied by the soloist or rhythm section. It should be noted from the outset that the most common variation in *harmonic rhythm* (the speed at which the chords change) is the delay of the final V chord until beat 3 of the 12th measure, so that the I chord, in effect, lasts for six beats, or one and a half measures. All of the examples in G that follow feature this delayed V (D7) chord.

There's something about the blues turnaround that allows and encourages the resourceful player to really make their mark and show off their individuality, creativity, and virtuosity. The shifting chords automatically create an interesting base to play over, more scales and interval choices are available, and the chords move by at a faster clip that provides contrast to the two- and four-measure chord durations that occur earlier in the form. Let's look at Winter's approach and see how the master handles these important situations.

This first turnaround lick begins in a fairly low register with Johnny approaching the root of the V chord (D7) from a half step below. Measure 2 begins with a hammered-on grace note, followed by a climb down the G blues scale to the root as measure 3 begins. He finishes with a classic phrase that includes a pitch-matching G-string bend, a descent through the G blues scale in the upper octave, and a final grace note into the major 3rd that drops down to low D. Stay in 3rd position throughout the example.

TRACK 19

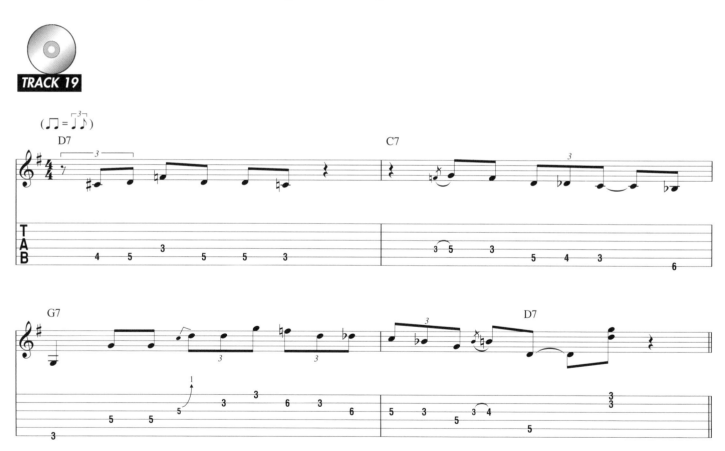

The next lick employs a little bit of rhythmic displacement, as the opening three-beat phrase is repeated in the 2nd measure but is pushed back a beat so that it begins on 2 rather than 1. In each instance, begin with a ring-finger pull-off on the B string and follow with a ring-finger slide-and-pull-off on the G string below. The final two measures combine the descending G blues scale with major and minor 3rds in close proximity before the phrase ends on an octave jump down from a high to a low D.

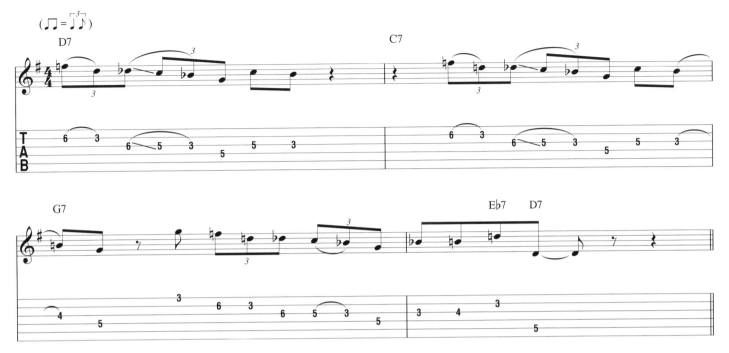

Here's a cool lick that features some string-skipping 6ths on the G and high E strings. Try playing the lower note with your middle finger and the higher note with your ring finger as you work your way down from the 7th fret to the 5th fret. Measure 3 brings us back to familiar territory with some blues scale triplets, and then the excerpt ends with the same move seen in the previous example: minor and major 3rds over the G7 chord and an octave jump down from high to low D. What's interesting to note about this lick is the way the descending 6ths seem to imply movement from D to C in *each* of the first two measures, providing a bit of conflict with the underlying chords (the B in measure 2 even clashes briefly with the B♭ in the C7 chord). Also note the nice use of chromaticism—the 6th-fret D♭s and B♭—to connect the 7th-fret intervals to those on the 5th fret.

TRACK 21

23

The parallel 6ths in the previous example get a bit more development in the phrase below and are played simultaneously as double stops rather than as individual notes. Try a hybrid picking approach here, with the pick, held normally, playing the lower notes, and your right-hand ring finger plucking the upper notes on the high E and B strings. Use your left-hand middle finger on the lower notes and your ring finger on the upper notes throughout. In measure 2, perform the upwards slide with your middle finger and the descending slide with your index finger; this will drop you down into 3rd position to begin measure 3.

TRACK 22

Next up is a classic turnaround lick with a comfortable, swinging rhythmic feel created by numerous triplets that really sit "in the pocket." It's pure, unadulterated Texas blues. Begin by alternating between your ring and middle fingers on the B and high E strings, respectively, jump down quickly to 3rd position, and then perform the first bend with your ring finger. Johnny returns to the pitch-matching motif seen earlier in measure 2, following up the G on the high E string with two B-string Gs played at the 8th fret. Measure 3 features a pre-bend–and–release on the high E string, while the final bar requires you to stretch down to the 3rd fret with your index finger to bring the lick to a tidy conclusion.

TRACK 23

The following example closely mirrors the previous one and again demonstrates Winter's willingness to return to and develop his strongest, most memorable ideas. Begin with the same triplet lick alternating between F and A, but end the opening measure by pulling off to the open G string. B♭ is once more bent up to C in measure 2, but this time we're in 3rd position and follow with a variation of the pitch-matching slide into G that should be quite familiar by now. Johnny returns to the pre-bending triplet phrase seen above in measure 3 and then ends the lick with another drop down to D. This time he stays in 6th position and adds a little ascending move to B♭.

TRACK 24

Here's a nice example of how to piece together some tried and true blues staples into a coherent and swinging turnaround lick. Begin with a series of triplets that starts with a pitch-matching bend and ends with a whole step bend on the high E string. Then there's the sliding move up the B string to the tonic in measure 2, the pre-bend–release–pull-off phrase seen earlier in measure 3, and then some three-note, barred chords in the final measure. When you have this lick and a fair amount of the earlier material under your fingers, try shuffling around these ideas and coming up with some solid turnaround phrases of your own. Use Johnny's playing as a jumping-off point, but be sure to put your own spin and personality into it. It's okay to mimic as you learn, but the ultimate goal should be the creation of a musical voice and playing style that's uniquely your own.

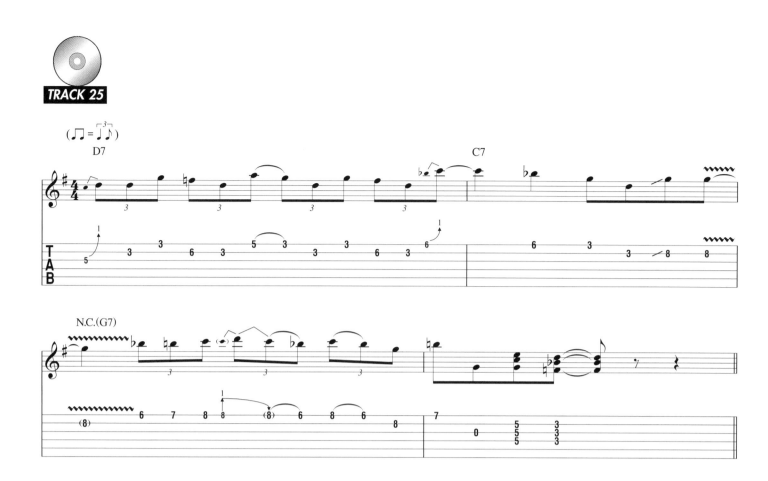

Let's return to the key of A and a straight eighth note feel for the final four licks in this chapter. The first begins in 5th position and, after a three-note pickup, alternates between the raised 9th (G) and 5th (B) of the E chord in much the same way as in the G blues turnarounds. Winter then slides up the G string into 10th position with his middle finger and outlines the D chord nicely by hitting its major 3rd (F♯) and bending into its ♭7th (C). Measure 3 begins with a slide down the B string that returns us to 5th position, where we finish out the lick with a stylish drop down to E at the A string's 7th fret.

TRACK 26

It should be clear by now that the G–B move that begins the next lick is a favorite of Johnny's, but he neverthe-less manages to keep things interesting by taking it to new places each time. In the 2nd measure, he slides up the G string into 10th position and lays down a sweet triplet phrase that climbs down the A blues scale before strik-ing the open G string and bending it up a whole step at the 7th fret. The 16th notes in the final measures pro-vide a nice rhythmic contrast with the triplets in measure 2.

Check out where Winter takes the next lick, which begins with the familiar G–B move and slides up into 10th position for the climb down the A blues scale once more. He "surrounds" the major 3rd, C♯, in measure 3, and then jumps all the way up to the 10th fret of the high E string before ending the lick with some tasty double stops. Play these with index- and ring-finger barres on the 5th and 7th frets, respectively, and use your middle finger for the quick grace-note hammer-on on the G string in the final measure.

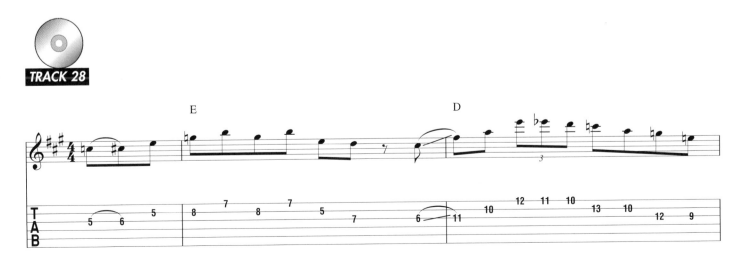

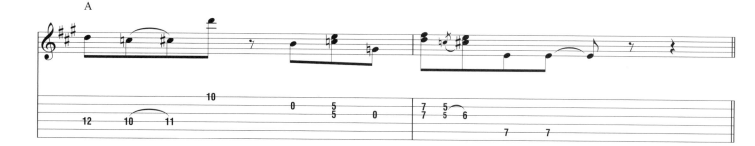

This last turnaround lick stays strictly within the 5th position, A blues scale box. Begin with a G-string bend and follow with some typical pull-off and hammer-on moves as you work your way down through the scale over the first two measures. The second half of the phrase begins with an octave jump up and includes both the minor (C) and major 3rd (C♯) of the tonic chord.

TRACK 29

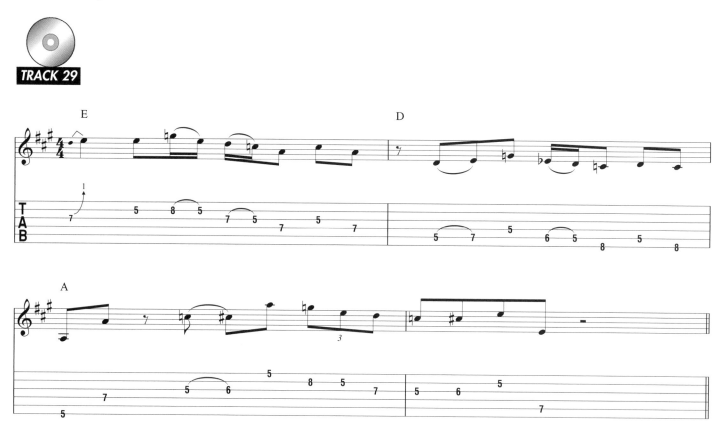

CODAS

In this short chapter, we'll check out four of Johnny's codas—free-form licks played over the tonic chord as a typical blues jam comes to its conclusion. The rhythms in these licks are fairly loose, as the band has stopped playing strict time and is instead hanging on the final chord while Winter does his thing.

This first example is in the key of G and begins in 3rd position. After the pickup, the major 3rd (B) is bent up a half step to C and followed by some typical riffing on the G blues scale. Later in the measure, the 4th (C) is bent up a half step to the ♭5th (D♭) and then released and pulled off to the minor 3rd (B♭) on the G string. Measure 3 includes some triplet-based permutations of the scale and finishes with an octave jump from low G to the middle register. The lick concludes with a double stop that combines the ♭7th (F) with the 9th (A) above and then two short hits on the tonic played on the low E string's 15th fret.

The lick below is also in G and begins in a similar way to our previous example, but quickly moves into fresh territory. While it stays in 3rd position throughout, variety is created by the combination of triplet and 16th note rhythms that also bring a nice sense of speed to the phrase. Winter implies a common blues chord sequence with the series of quarter notes that begins in measure 3. The G–F to the C and E double-stop in measure 4 clearly outlines the (I–I7–IV) progression (here, G–G7–C) that is often heard at the end of the blues and may be followed by a C minor chord (iv) before returning to the I chord. Interestingly, Johnny ends the example by sliding down from a high A9 chord rather than hitting the tonic.

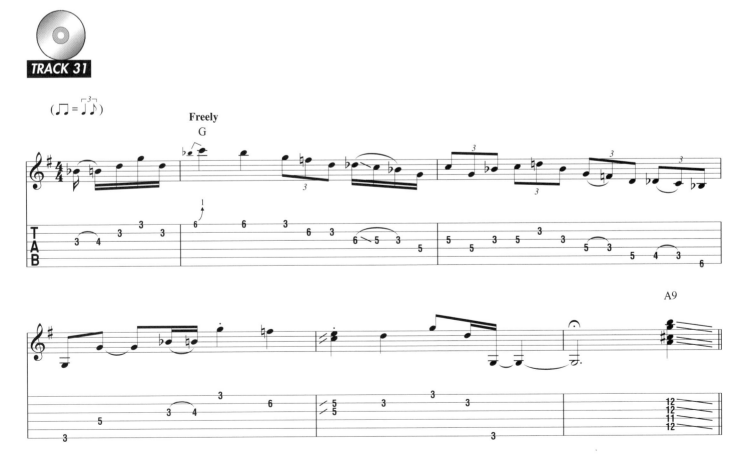

This next example is up a whole step in the key of A. After sliding up the G string to the major 3rd (C♯), Winter returns to familiar territory with some 5th-position A blues scale moves, including the whole step bend from the minor 3rd (C) to the 4th (D), and the bend–release–pull-off on the G string at the end of the 1st measure. He also demonstrates once again the authentic blues flavor that can be created by including the major 3rd in close juxtaposition with the minor 3rd—it can create a sense of resolution on its own. The intriguing tritone interval that exists between the 3rd and the ♭7th can be heard near the end of the phrase before Johnny puts a cap on the whole thing by landing emphatically on the root and sliding down.

TRACK 32

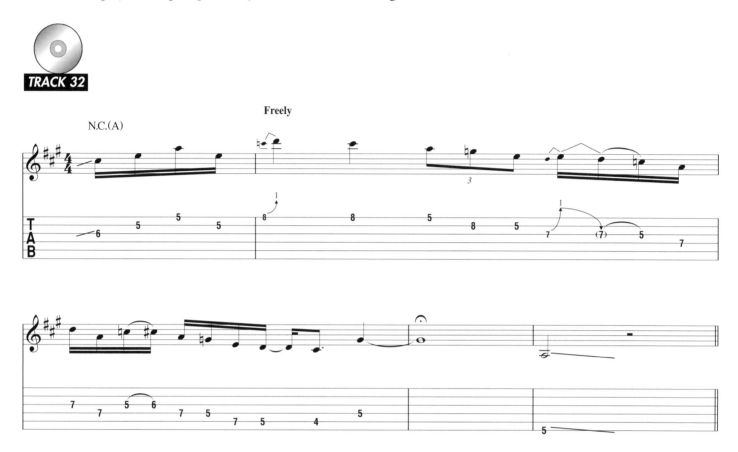

This final coda lick is in the key of E and begins with a ring-finger slide up the B string to the 5th fret, putting us in 3rd position. The half step bend on the high E string should be played with the ring finger as well. The inclusion of the open high E string (2nd beat of the 1st measure) allows us to drop down into open position and finish out the lick there, using the middle finger to perform the downwards grace-note slide from B♭ to A and the pull-off to the open G string. Notice that Winter once again ends a phrase with the combination of the ♭7th (D) and the 9th above it (F♯) while striking the open low E string as the two higher notes continue to ring.

TRACK 33

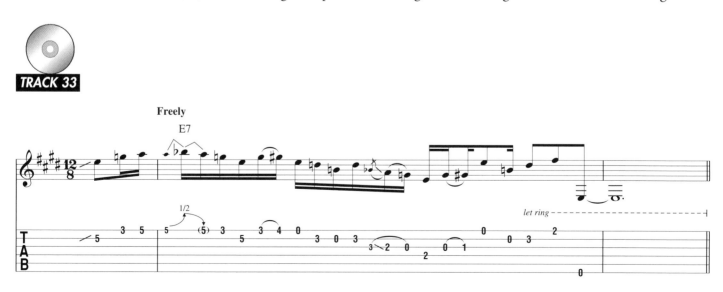

12-BAR SOLOS

We now turn our attention to a handful of Johnny's complete choruses, each lasting for a full cycle through the 12-bar blues form and giving us a chance to examine the ways in which he strings together his licks into cohesive and memorable statements. After working your way through this chapter and learning the way the master does it, try composing some of your own 12-bar solos. While the blues is largely an improvisatory style, and should ideally be approached with a sense of freedom and exploration, having a stockpile of licks, tricks, and complete solos under your fingers gives you more ammunition to draw from or to use as a jumping off point in live performances. The more prepared you are in terms of both guitar technique and stylistic vocabulary, the more you'll be free to pursue the music in your ears instead of simply running your fingers, hoping to luck into something good!

This first solo is in the key of A and is played with a funky, straight eighth note feel. Winter begins with a low-register riff figure in 5th position, built on the A minor pentatonic scale. As we move to the IV chord (D), he introduces the ♭5th (E♭) but remains in the same position, sticking to the lowest three strings. Upon returning to the tonic chord in measure 7, he works his way into higher registers—sliding up the B string with the ring finger to the 10th fret—and lands in 8th position, where he remains for much of the next two measures. Play the 10th-fret bends on both the high E and B strings with your ring finger here and use your pinky to get to the high D in measure 9. Move up to 10th position in measure 10 and then slide back down the B string with your index finger to 5th position for the last two measures. The two double stops at the solo's end should be played with your index and middle fingers on the D and B strings, respectively.

TRACK 34

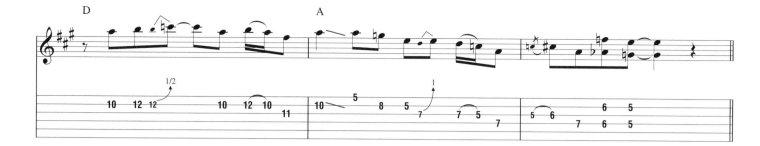

The next three solos are in E and return to the slow 12/8 time signature used for the previous examples in this key. The example below beautifully illustrates Winter's approach to solo blues playing, as he provides his own accompaniment by moving seamlessly between low-register riffing, open-string licks, and higher-register ideas. This is an approach worth having for any guitarist, and one that takes time to develop. Try simply hitting a chord on the downbeat of each measure and following with a single-note lick over the beats that follow. After a bit of practicing, you should be able to make things rhythmically more complex and develop your own methods of integrating solo and accompaniment without running into too many obstacles. Winter begins this solo with a familiar blues riff on the low E and A strings (another nice starting point to try) and gradually introduces higher-register notes to the mix while maintaining the groove at all times. In measure 4, he jumps up to 7th position, using his index finger on the high E string and middle finger for the Gs on the B string below. The quarter tone bends indicate a slight push upwards that should never quite reach G♯. Use your index finger to slide back down the A string to the 2nd fret at the end of the measure as you approach the IV chord (A7). Winter returns to the quarter step B-string bends at the end of measure 8, moves to 5th position in measure 9, and then finishes out the solo with some classic moves combining open strings and fretted notes. The "tr" above the final note (A) indicates a trill—in this case, rapid hammer-ons and pull-offs between the open A string and the B at its 2nd fret. Use your strongest digit, the index finger, and simply move back and forth as quickly as possible for the duration of the dotted quarter note (three beats in 12/8).

TRACK 35

32

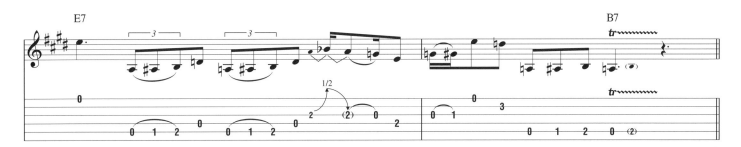

This next solo, packed densely with chords, shows us that we don't always need to play a lot of fast single-note licks to make a real impact. If you're familiar with even a fraction of Winter's recorded output, you *know* he can spit out blazing, machine-gun lines till the cows come home, but he also knows enough about the genre to recognize it isn't purely a vehicle for virtuoso grandstanders. Johnny doesn't need to prove his mettle to anyone, so he relaxes instead and demonstrates an easygoing, jazz-inflected chorus full of chromatic chord movements. After the initial ring-finger slide up the G string, he flattens the finger into a barre across the top three strings, adds his index and middle fingers to the D and A strings, respectively, and repeats the ensuing E9 chord until the end of the measure, when he moves the shape up a fret at a time to connect chromatically with the A9 chord in measure 2. This shift to the IV (often referred to as the *fast IV*) is temporary, however, and he performs another chromatic maneuver back down to the tonic at the end of the measure. Winter keeps things interesting by moving up a half step to an F9 chord here, adding and removing the 13th (D on the high E string's 10th fret) with his pinky, and then continues up to F♯9 before working his was back down to the E9 chord. The half step up move is common enough, but the jump up to F♯9 is fairly unusual and not something you'd want to do with a band unless you've worked it out ahead of time with the other players. Playing alone, however, affords the guitarist ample opportunity to add chord substitutions at whim. In measures 5 and 6, Johnny drops down into open position and plays a simple single-note lick on the B and high E strings and then follows up with a series of three- and four-note chords in measures 7 and 8. Here, he uses a rootless E7 inversion, drops an inverted B7 chord into the mix, and adds barre shapes on the top three strings in measure 8. The temporary move to the V chord (B7) is another common substitution that is used, like the "fast IV" in measure 2, to break up the monotony in a slow blues setting. The final four measures employ string-skipping single-note lines exclusively. Take note of the implied progression in the final two measures: E–E7–A/C♯–Am/C–E/B–B7. This chord sequence is heard all the time in blues bass and/or keyboard parts but is frequently ignored by guitarists. It's an important part of the turnaround that should be learned in all keys for a more authentic approach to the style.

Our last 12-bar solo expands on many of the same ideas seen in the previous example. Begin with the inverted E7 shape seen earlier on the three top strings, and then move the shape down a fret in measure 2 to an implied E diminished chord (or an A7♭9, depending on your perspective). Measure 4 includes the higher-register barre shapes encountered above, shifting chromatically down and then upwards, leading into the A9 chord in measure 5.

Winter climbs back down a fret at a time in measure 6 and lays down some classic open-string licks in the measures that follow. The last two measures bring back the turnaround progression from the previous solo in a new way: with a series of double stops spread between the D and high E strings. Use a hybrid picking approach here, plucking the D-string notes with the pick and the high E-string notes with your right-hand ring finger.

Slide Licks in Alternate Tunings

In the second half of this book, we'll switch gears and examine Johnny Winter's slide guitar style in three different tunings: open G, open D, and "open F♯," which is open D up two whole steps. Many of these licks were recorded on a National-style resonator guitar. If you're unfamiliar with slide guitar technique, you may want to do a bit of remedial work, as it's an advanced and highly specialized art that requires practice and study before one can pull it off with a reasonable degree of competence and confidence. While the tremendous range of slide guitar techniques and tricks falls beyond the scope of this book, here are a few pointers to consider before jumping into the world of bluesy, bottleneck bliss.

1. Johnny wears a thin steel slide on the pinky of his fretting hand. This allows him to lift the slide away from the fretboard and use his other fingers to fret notes in the normal way. Experiment with different slides—glass is another popular option—and fingers. Many players wear the slide on the ring finger, but this may limit your options when playing normally. Winter often uses a ring-style fingerpick when playing slide as well.

2. The string height of your guitar will either help or hinder your slide playing tremendously. While low action is preferable for normal playing and makes everything easier to pull off, this kind of setup makes slide playing difficult. The slide should be held above the fret wire rather than in between the frets (i.e., over the wood). It should also be laid on a string gently, without pushing down. Low string height will likely make it hard to avoid hitting the frets and choking your notes off, so chose a guitar with moderate to high action.

3. Dampen the unused strings with both hands. Try flattening one or more of your slide-hand fingers onto the strings behind the slide as you move up and down to avoid excessive whines and overtones. The index finger is the easiest to use in this fashion. The picking hand should be used in a similar way, with the non-picking fingers and palm muting the unused strings. You don't want to hear the slide running over the A string while you're playing a lick on the G string! If you hold your pick in the traditional way (between thumb and forefinger), your middle finger can mute the B string and the side of your thumb can dampen the A and D strings when playing a G-string lick.

4. Alternate tuning rearranges the fretboard, obviously, so take some time to learn where the notes are in each new tuning and how you can use this information to your advantage. Triads and power chords can usually be played with the slide simply barring the strings, and scales are often contained within a fret or two of the tonic. Some slide guitarists play in standard tuning, allowing them to see the fretboard in the normal way and get to more harmonically complex ideas—Warren Haynes is a good example of a player in this style. But most players, including Johnny Winter, employ alternate tunings extensively when using their slides. At minimum, learn to play your pentatonic scales on the first five frets in both open G and open D tunings.

5. Solid intonation is crucial when playing slide and may take some time to develop. Remember that the slide needs to hit the string squarely above the fret to be in tune. Vibrato in slide playing can help pull your pitches into tune, since it is created by moving the slide back and forth horizontally, instead of by making small vertical bends. Be sure to play over some recorded chord progressions or with friends so you can hear whether you're hitting your marks or not in terms of intonation.

OPEN G TUNING

The examples in this chapter are all played in open G tuning, so be sure to tune your guitar strings, low to high, D–G–D–G–B–D before you get started. From your low E to your high E string, this will give you the 5th, root, 5th, root, 3rd, and 5th of a G major chord on your open strings.

TRACK 38

Open G tuning, low to high: D–G–D–G–B–D

Johnny played the examples in this chapter on his National resonator guitar.

This first lick can be played over the tonic chord (G) in the first four measures of a blues. Begin by sliding into the 12th fret of the high E string from slightly below, making sure to hit the 5th of the G chord, and then slide from the 11th to the 12th fret on the B string, thereby moving from the minor 3rd to the major 3rd (B♭ to B). After playing the root at the G string's 12th fret, slide down the neck and use the slide to play the B♭ at the 3rd fret of the A string. You'll return to this idea in the 2nd and 3rd measures, with slight variations each time. By the end of measure 3, you're done with the early higher-register ideas; you finish out the phrase with pentatonic ideas using open strings and notes on the 1st, 3rd, and 5th frets. Apply vibrato to the last note of the example by moving the slide back and forth horizontally a short distance along the D string. Move too far and you'll pull the note out of tune rather than giving it the characteristic vibrato that's called for. Take note of the various ways the slide is used here and in other examples. Sometimes you should play the note indicated by landing on it squarely with no sliding action, sometimes you should connect one note to another by sliding, and at other times you should slide into the note from a few frets below. Be careful not to exaggerate the distance of each slide unless otherwise indicated, as this will create a goofy and undesirable effect. Control is key!

TRACK 39

This next lick is a loose turnaround with a bit of an extension at the end. The phrase still begins in measure 9 of the 12-bar blues form, but two bars are added to the total since it's played as the actual ending of a performance and does not continue into a fresh chorus. Winter begins with a repeated phrase that moves from the open A string to the 3rd fret, goes up to the open D string, and then slides into a higher pitch (either A or G). With a lick like this, you need to make sure that you bring the slide down on the string *gently* without banging into the fret so that the transition between open-string and slide notes isn't too jarring and your volume remains consistent. Near the end of the phrase, Johnny adds a descending chord figure that is played without the slide—simply lift your pinky away from the neck and fret the low E-string notes normally. Once again, apply vibrato carefully where indicated. Johnny is a master here, and often appears to be wiggling the slide wildly, but the sound he produces is always tasteful and controlled. Keep your movements small to be on the safe side. Once you have the technique under your fingers, you can adjust as you see fit.

TRACK 40

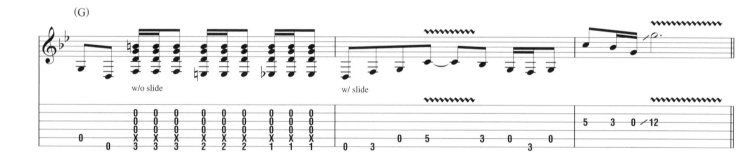

The excerpt below constitutes another full 12-bar blues chorus. You may want to work on this in two-measure chunks and reassemble the whole later, as Johnny jumps around the neck a good deal and plays some choice phrases in each region. He begins with the slide on the 12th fret and descends from the high E string to the B and G strings over the first two bars. He follows this by dropping down the neck and adding some tasty pentatonic lines within the first five frets. In measure 5, he clearly outlines the IV chord (C) and then performs a long slide up the high E string from the 2nd to the 10th fret before sliding back down into the lower frets and mixing in carefully chosen open strings. The turnaround, beginning in measure 9, outlines the V chord (D) and mimics the 5th-fret barred C-chord lick heard earlier.

39

Here's another 12-bar solo chock full of fascinating, authentic blues phrases. Much of the action takes place within the first five frets of the neck and employs open strings extensively. If you've done your homework and learned the locations of all of the notes in open G tuning, you'll be in good shape to jump in and observe just how much music Johnny milks from this area of the fretboard. Notice how he returns yet again to the 5th-fret barre idea heard in the previous example as the action shifts to the IV chord (C) in measure 5. This is followed up by sliding double stops on the B and high E strings that ultimately move you into the 12th-fret region of the neck. The remainder of the solo is played back down on the lower frets and features a number of pitch-matching slides in which the open G string is followed by a slide into the 5th fret of the D string. These can also be heard in the first two measures, giving the solo a nice sense of cohesion and order.

TRACK 42

This final 12-bar example in open G tuning is the most challenging yet, and features a handful of new moves and numerous register leaps. Begin in the lower regions of the neck and perform repeated G-string pull-offs with the slide in the first three measures. Using the slide to pull off to an open string is a bit different from performing a standard pull-off, which usually includes a subtle pull towards the floor as you lift your finger from the neck. With the slide, you merely play the indicated note and then lift away to sound the open string. The six pull-offs here give you ample opportunities to practice this technique, which requires just enough force to sound both the slide note and the open string without noisily banging down onto the fret. Sliding down very slightly as you pull off may help as well. Measure 4 includes slides from the ♭5th up to the perfect 5th as well as the major 3rd on the open B string, while measure 5 returns you to the C-triad shape found across the 5th frets of the G, B, and high E strings. A series of barred double stops follows—beginning with a pull-off to the open B and high E strings—and climbs up and down the neck. You'll move as high as the 15th fret in measure 8—a tricky maneuver if performed on an acoustic instrument without a cutaway. The turnaround slides you up to the 7th fret as you outline a D triad, descends from repeated 12th-fret Ds on the high E string in measure 10, and then drops down into the lower register for a chromatic climb from the minor 3rd (B♭) to the 5th (D), one fret at a time.

TRACK 43

OPEN D TUNING

All of the licks in this short chapter were played by Johnny on his Gibson Firebird solidbody electric in open D tuning. This commonly used alternate tuning (low to high: D–A–D–F♯–A–D) is fairly similar to open G and includes, from low to high, the root, 5th, root, 3rd, 5th, and root of a D major chord on the open strings.

TRACK 44

Open D tuning, low to high: D–A–D–F♯–A–D

Having the root on the outer strings (low and high E) makes it a little bit easier to navigate, but you should still take your time learning the placement of the D minor pentatonic scale notes on each string. Open D is often tuned up a whole step to open E (E–B–E–G♯–B–E) in the work of players such as Duane Allman and Derek Trucks, and up two whole steps to open F♯ by Johnny Winter in the final chapter of this book. Needless to say, the following licks are merely the tip of the iceberg in terms of what can be done in this tuning, but they should provide you with a strong starting point for further exploration.

This first phrase moves chromatically up the B string from the 4th (G) to the flat and perfect 5ths (G♯ and A) before finishing up on a vibrato-laden D at the 12th fret of the high E string. Remember to drag your slide-hand index finger behind the bottleneck to dampen the unused strings. Experiment with pick-hand dampening as well; your middle finger can mute the high E string while you play the B string, and the side of your thumb can be used to dampen the G string below.

TRACK 45

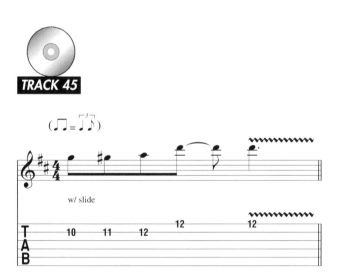

This next example packs a lot of cool ideas into a few short measures and hits nearly all of the most crucial areas in open D tuning. The first half of the phrase explores the territory between the open strings and the 5th fret and clearly illustrates the placement of the D minor pentatonic scale notes in this region. Later, you move up the neck and mine the area between the 10th and 12th frets, sliding into the major 3rd (F♯ at the G string's 12th fret) in measure 3 and outlining the D major triad. Note the placement of the minor 3rd (F) and 4th (G) as well, and the contrasting major pentatonic sounds (E and F♯) at the end of the lick.

Here's another loosely played phrase full of beautiful and authentic open D licks. Although this lick includes many of the places visited in the earlier examples—pentatonic notes on the bottom five frets and open strings, the 12th-fret triad tones, etc.—there are also the root and minor 3rd on the 8th frets of the G and B strings, respectively. The G–F–D idea that begins at the end of measure 1 is repeated twice in measure 5 before the example reaches its conclusion.

TRACK 47

Let's finish this short introduction to open D tuning with an exciting 12-bar electric blues solo. It bears repeating that this material is more than the sum of its parts. Winter isn't just stringing together his favorite licks—he's telling a musical story with all of the requisite ingredients. By all means break the example up into chunks and learn it a measure or two at a time, but remember when you reassemble its constituent pieces that it's a complete and fully realized musical statement that flows naturally and inevitably from one measure to the next.

The first four measures include a number of slides and pull-offs on the high E string that demand careful execution. In the case of the former, it's essential that you hit your marks cleanly to avoid pulling your notes out of tune, while in the latter you'll need just the right amount of force to sound the open E string without "dinking" the fret wire with the slide. The long slide from the 3rd fret to the 9th fret and back down again in measure 4 is particularly tricky. As you work your way through the rest of the solo, take note of all of the little details that add up to make such a significant impact. Slides of varying lengths are used to approach notes from both below and above, while vibrato is employed economically to great effect. The final four measures feature a particularly tasty turnaround phrase worthy of a place in any blues musician's arsenal.

TRACK 48

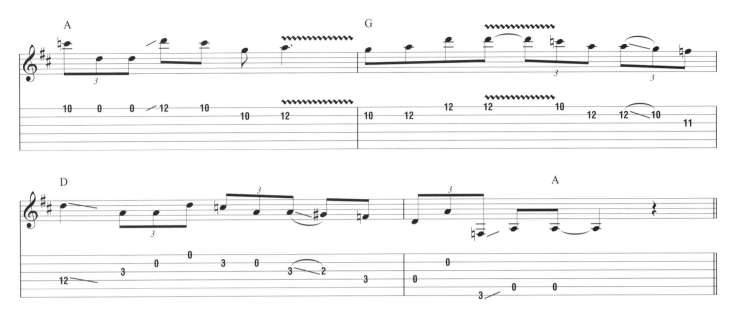

"OPEN F♯" TUNING

All of the licks in this final chapter were recorded by Johnny on a National resonator guitar, tuned to open D up two whole steps so the strings sound F♯–C♯–F♯–A♯–C♯–F♯, low to high. To play along with the recordings, simply tune to open D (low to high: D–A–D–F♯–A–D) using the pitches in track 44, capo at the 4th fret, and play the examples as written. The higher string tension of the F♯ tuning results in a more pronounced attack and stinging sound to the notes. Be careful if you're attempting the F♯ tuning on a standard guitar, as the neck will be under a lot of strain and you may snap a string or two in the process. Try a very light gauge if you insist!

Let's take a look at a few short licks Johnny favors in this tuning. The standard notation below reflects the open D tuning but does not include the shift up two whole steps, so that the open high E string is shown as a D, rather than the F♯ you will hear if tuned up accordingly. The first phrase begins with the open low E string and then moves around between the 5th fret and open strings in the higher registers. This should look somewhat familiar if you worked your way through the previous chapter on open D tuning.

TRACK 50

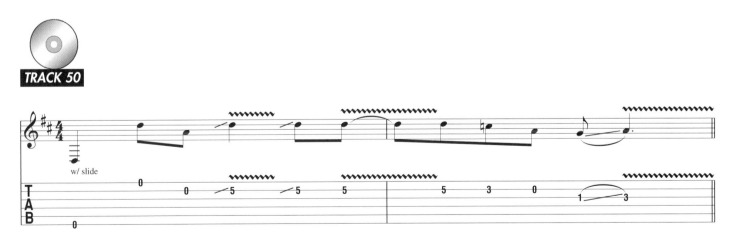

Here's a simple and tasty lick on the A and low E strings. Notice that it includes all of the pitches of a minor pentatonic scale as it moves between the 5th fret, 3rd fret, and open E and A strings. Again, don't be thrown off by the standard notation, which shows the phrase in D rather than F♯.

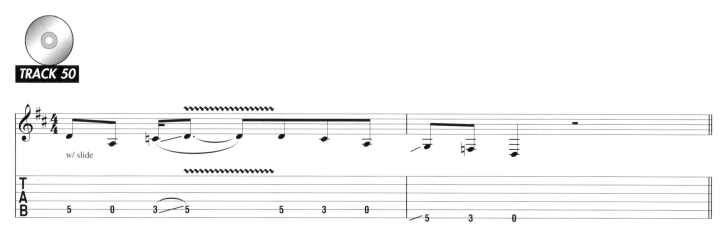

The next lick includes slides both up and down between the 1st and 3rd frets on the G string. Playing so close to the nut can be a little tricky, as your string height is likely to be at its lowest in this region and slide-hand dampening becomes impossible. You'll need to do some extra work with your pick hand to keep this one sounding clean.

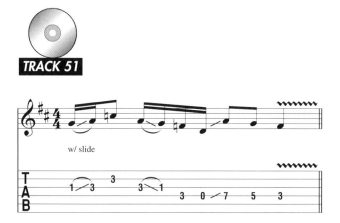

The lick below provides a nice mix of 16th notes and eighth notes, and demonstrates how to mix open strings effectively with a few choice fretted tones. The second double stop in measure 2 is a bit tricky to manage, as you need to be careful not to hit the open G string with the top of the slide as you play the B string's 3rd fret.

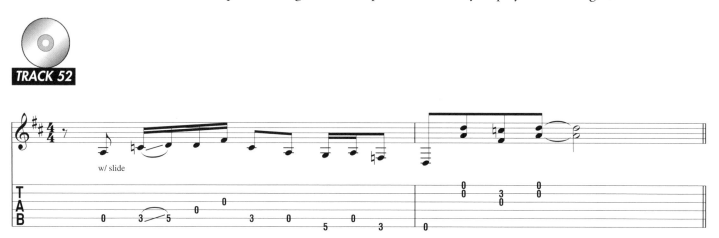

Here's a longer lick that mixes eighth notes with soulful slides into quarter note triplets. Throw this one into a slow blues solo for a bit of that authentic, old-school bottleneck sound. The heavy vibrato mimics the plaintive vocal wail of the Delta bluesmen of old.

Here's a higher-register lick—centered around the 12th-fret triad and its surrounding tones—that is similar to phrases examined in the open D tuning chapter. The open F♯ tuning, with its increased string tension, really gives this one some bite. Try to exaggerate the vibrato by moving your hand back and forth very quickly without allowing the slide to drift too far in either direction. Once again, this mimics the technique of vocalists who use vibrato to pull themselves into tune and keep themselves there on sustained pitches. Vibrato can also be used to correct slight intonation problems on the fly, but it should not be used as a substitute for accurate slide work in the long run.

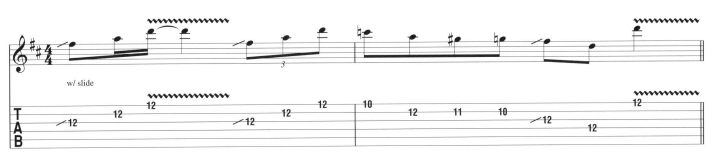

The lick below continues the exploration of open-string possibilities, combining these notes with tones on the 1st fret of the G string and 3rd frets of the D, G, and B strings. In measure 3, perform the half step bends on the B string with your ring finger while lifting the slide away from the neck. Fretting notes normally while wearing the slide on the pinky may take some getting used to, so you may want to practice playing lines and even chords while wearing it and holding it away from the fretboard. Once you've gotten comfortable with this technique, you'll be able to switch between fretted notes, chords, and slide work quickly, greatly enhancing your versatility and sonic palette.

The following four-measure phrase contrasts upper-register tones on the 12th fret and surrounding areas with low-register ideas on the open strings and first five frets. Many of the classic blues concepts Winter employs throughout this book are on display here, including the combination of minor and major sounds, and pitch-matching phrases, such as the open D-string and 5th-fret A-string notes found in the final measure.

This final example uses chords extensively and requires you to hold the slide away from the neck while fretting notes normally. In fact, the only note you should play with the slide is the 5th fret of the low E string on beat 4 of the 2nd measure. The five-note chords in measures 1 and 4 should be played with your index and middle fingers on the B and high E strings, respectively. The 3rd-fret notes in measure 2 should be played with the middle finger, while you'll need to adopt a hybrid-picking approach in measure 3, grabbing the open high E string with your ring finger while using the pick to strike the two notes on the G string. All in all, this one should provide an excellent opportunity to practice standard playing while wearing the slide on your fretting hand—an admittedly awkward technique when first attempted. Good luck!

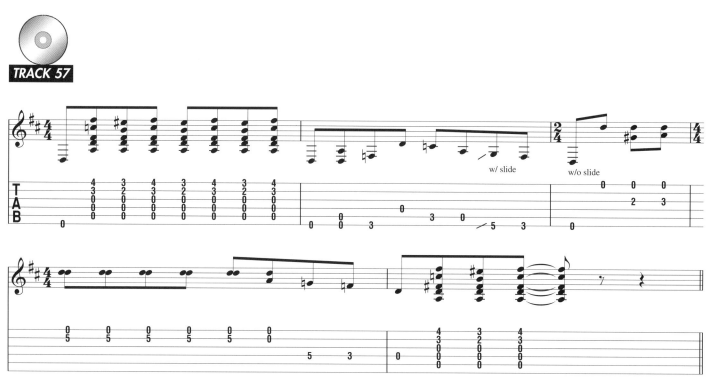

We've come to the end of our blues lessons here, but this may only be the beginning of your explorations of the style and of the work of Johnny Winter in particular. I urge you to continue your studies, not only of this great player but also of his many important influences and forebears. The blues is a musical genre rich in tradition and history; it reflects the experiences and struggles of African Americans in the United States, and the joys and pains of their daily lives. It is a music that informs nearly all of the contemporary styles heard in the Western world. Its pantheon is full of unique characters who carried on the work of previous generations while adding their own sounds and styles to the canon. Unearth the work of these artists as you do your part to push the style ahead in your own time. Learn from the past, but let your own artistry shine through and shape the future of the blues.